BRUISED GOSPEL

Copyright © 2020 by Sarah Alcaide-Escue

Bruised Gospel

ISBN 978-1-7328741-2-1

First Edition

Typeset in Rosarivo

The Lune
Fort Collins, CO
www.poetsonearth.com

BRUISED GOSPEL

Sarah Alcaide-Escue

Homonyms for Separation from Origin	7
Migrant Speech	9
On Nights When I Am Motherless	10
After Your Funeral	11
Winter	12
Shell	13
June	15
Spirit Bear	21
I Bloom Like Ginger Root	22
Ode to Sapria Himalayana	23
After Meditating in the Forest	24
The Coyote in Chiang Mai, Mile 19	25
Tsuku Tsuku Boshi	26
Requiem for the Northern Forest	27
Portrait of Myself as the Hillsborough River, Late September	28
Mid-summer	29
Your Heart is an Empty Church	35
Believe In What It Isn't	36
Self-Portrait with Fire	37
The Darker Half of the Year	38
The Ungardening	39
August in Georgia is a Pigeon-Pale Blooming	40
Tongue, Endangered	41
Litany of Departures	42

I

And where does he go,
that shadowy figure who handles my memories?

CHLOE HONUM

HOMONYMS FOR SEPARATION FROM ORIGIN

calving (v.):   1. as in, to give birth to a calf
                    2. of a glacier or iceberg, to break off
                                                  or detach

                        ::

cow in the snow
her blood   her body's halo

                  suckling still sucking milk

                                      too late to be unbroken

                        ::

birth of noun   birth of mountain
        cold placenta

                              Mother, I'm fractured (crevice or crevasse?)

                        ::

the motherless calf straggles through ice fields
the snow falls   muddling the mudling

                        ::

I crawl
inside my second body— a place to pray   a place to hide
                         a place to remember the sound of
                                              your voice, mother:

                                    hush
                                         hush
                                              hush—

                              ::

the only part of you left   (me)

hours shift
into a dark thaw

MIGRANT SPEECH

tilt of summer
face full of flies

my mind   unwinds
sheds   as a serpent
my illness   can't be held
can't bleed   but rather ripens
rots   like speech

now the wind
          now shadowplay on pavement

i want a name
for everything—   why

my tongue   unhinges
pries   from the dry throats of strangers   sound

i mispronounce my name
those simple syllables
but still re-   assemble this body
               each mourning

perhaps i am stronger   than the ground   i was cut from

ON NIGHTS WHEN I AM MOTHERLESS

Through the limbs of an ash tree,
ash filters, reminds me of the nights
we watched the storm from the front door,

your cigarette smoke blown through the screen.
Tonight, the mutt's holler rolls over hills
like a tongue over unbrushed teeth.

A wolf spider spins a gossamer hammock,
carries her young on her back, eats them.
The moon unhinges from its socket.

Still, your silhouette shrinks
in the sky-stone's sheen.
Still, the petals of the crocus close,
unable to wake 'til morning.

AFTER YOUR FUNERAL

I throw your leather jacket,
your sheets, your handwritten
letters, into the river.

Broken wine bottles stud
the river's cusp, glass shards
slice the sky, drawing blood—
thick drops blot my skin
like cigarette burns on a car seat.

Our rope swing strings
that tree—tattered, unspooling.

You're the thick pill
I can't swallow,
the cyst in my esophagus.

You, the sore
I can't quit tonguing.

The prayer I recite before sleep—

I slip into rust-red water,
sink in the mud.

WINTER

kisses the bougainvillea.

      Blood-orange bracts crack and curl,
                              cling
                                      to bowing thorny branches

until   one

          by one

               they fall
                      atop grass blades brittle in the garden's nape.

I gape at each paper-petal
                unfurling
                              from its mother.

I wonder, who will admire me   in death?

SHELL

Drape me in that palm's shade,
I'm a flesh-sack
with no map to my organs.

Do you know where I left
the blood-pumping fist
that fits beneath my ribs?

I think I lost it in your apartment
last year, after I smashed
the television with your mother's

vintage lamp.
The doctor says these pills
will sanitize my cerebrum,

untwist my tongue.
Will it be enough
to remind me of the woman I was—

folded hands, pressed dress,
lips locked tight like a rosebud?
A cow carcass roadside is a shell.

I'm glass shattered.
Mosaic me into something
beautiful, inhuman—

a dropped nightgown on hardwood.
An afternoon's ripe hue,
the apse of a child's elbow.

JUNE

After Chloe Honum

Father tried to take his life.
Moths circled lamplight,
their wings uneven shadows.

Our half-lit home,
a babbling child.
Empty pantry, spoiled milk,

the stove left lit
while everyone slept,
cigarette burns on sheets.

I watched him
from the kitchen window,
my father. His clothes wet

from walking into the river.
Still, our neighborhood tilted
at the river's divide,

unstitched earth's seam.
Seasons end & begin & end,
suturing each breath.

How briefly are we blameless?

II

She hears voices from under the earth.

SUSAN GRIFFIN

SPIRIT BEAR

    Great Bear Rainforest, British Columbia

hours unfold
autumn's shadowy figure
                raw season   of fish glut   pink rot
                rain patch   & rockweed

miles of streamside rock   silhouette of tidal sedge

Moksgm'ol paws salmon   chews cedar bark   each movement fringed—
spirit hunted by smoke

far off   the fishing village echoes   ravens mills canneries—
a territory of mouths

        this mother   island soft & muted holsters
                                                hemlock & yew
interrupts river with rock

        still unnamed shapes   slit silver bellies of fish   suck out eggs

teeth take   until blue's boot prints   fade gray

I BLOOM LIKE GINGER ROOT

Morning, old friend, has fallen into trees,

    collects in the forest's corner like dust.

Rooting red earth, ginger blooms,

    and so do I—petals yellow,

unfold for the sun-sprawled sky.

    There's a boiling beneath my thread-

thin roots—earth's call to be unburied, rediscovered.

    Wind whispers to each of my leaves

in a language I don't recognize. I dig

    my feet deeper, stretch out

my greening stems in search of words.

ODE TO SAPRIA HIMALAYANA

lo the bloodsucker's globuse body   how she buds from the earth like a recurring dream
lo her claret-red flesh with spots sulfur-yellow ::   a jewel sprouting from the vine
lo how this campanulate parasite lodges herself
                lozenge-like in the mountain's shadow-throat

     as a leopard lingers in the riverdark   she too waits with mouth agape
               to suck the root of *tetrastigma*—   lianas unclasping themselves
                          from the forest floor like bloated leeches from veins

                    o   how   i admire *sapria*'s unhinged jaws
                          her anointing pigsty stench of fruit rot

                                         bejewelled & buried with the memory of greener fields
                                         where i slip   beyond the boundary of dreaming & not

o how i wish i could ossify
like other hollow-boned babes

       like the red-wingèd fowl falls
           mid-flight   whose feathers unthread from flesh

i will be reborn as hungry
i will shed my shape to hold the weight of every dying thing—

               a body apostrophed

                                               translated into light

AFTER MEDITATING IN THE FOREST

A wind filters through me,
        my lungs swell, unswell.

Buried beneath my body,
        another earth un-
spools, silk from a spindle.

Still, the bird   song rises,
        not like river   water
rises in a flood, nor steam
from a teacup   like a prayer.

Pines yellow,
        huddle to warm
themselves in the rain.

The moon is an organ, a spider—
sclerotic,
        dang-
                ling
from its own   web.

Seeds root & sprout,
  vines twist around my rib cage.
Frog rattle, wounded doe—
  I dissolve back into the earth.

THE COYOTE IN CHIANG MAI, MILE 19

Tonight: an upturned *phayom* canoe.
A crocodile carcass laps the lakeside,
skin split open, filaments unthreading.

A crane unhooks its beak
from the rat's neck. Ember-eyed,
a coyote struts through the thicket,
tongue hanging in half-howl.

Then, me: the émigré, the stray.

Night, the great scavenger,
necklaces our fleshy caverns,
picks and licks us clean.

By a man's hands the coyote's hulk
is hollowed, its silk belly unravels.

How we look the same in the dark,
the coyote and I, and the entrails—
spilling out onto the earth,
silhouettes snaking in dusk.

TSUKU TSUKU BOSHI

Undress me
slowly.

Undress me slowly
like cicadas undress

sweaty cobalt skies late-July.
Do you hear their sheath-

tymbals unbuckle and click?
Children unpin

from scarred limbs socks.
Tree crickets sip

root-sap with straws,
chirr summer to sleep.

Dusk pinks. We wither,
we wane, like a garden.

Will we return unfurled,
as the chrysanthemums
skirting the city?

REQUIEM FOR THE NORTHERN FOREST

Winter buries me
        with wind-worn hands,

unhinges my jaw.
        My body is a landfill,

it glints like the mount at sunfall.
        Dusk-hushed, a moth thumps

athwart the porch
        light, folds into dust.

I burrow inside
        my second skin—sanctuary

of painted glass and stone.
        Mid-eclipse, the moon rusts,

hangs above sallow pines.
        Still, a hyacinth purples

in the ice field, survives
        the snowstorm strong-stemmed.

Every day, I pray for color, growth,
        but every day I sink deeper in snow.

PORTRAIT OF MYSELF AS THE HILLSBOROUGH RIVER,
LATE SEPTEMBER

Autumn spills, stains my body
gourd-orange with the maple's leaves.

Limpkins shrill & preen on a cypress's knee.
With each click of wind, cattails copper & quill.

Sunlight drapes bare branches like moss,
clings to silken threads spun by a lone spider.

Limpkins shrill louder still.
Afternoon, a stone, falls

& shatters my surface like bone.
And do you hear the lilies?

They whirr with each brush of fin, asking:
When, from the mud, will we unroot?

MIDSUMMER

you're taller now   sequoia
but i'm taller

how else can i write
the mountain or the river   silvering in snow—
how else can i dis assemble   language

enough to crawl inside silos   filled with wheat

i don't need your permission
    i will bury myself
beneath layers of grain   dust

no one   not even you   will find me

III

To know love that was beyond an owning, beyond
the body and its needs, but went straight from wild
thing to wild thing, approving of its wildness.

ADA LIMÓN

YOUR HEART IS AN EMPTY CHURCH

Couched on ripped pews, we inhale
sticky-sweet smoke—electric citrus,
summer thunder, liquid cinnamon.

Your name dissolves
on my tongue—a velvet fig.
I bathe you

in the baptistery,
dip your feet in cedarwood oil.
On the rooftop, we share the last

bottle of wine. Ripe lips stain
naked thighs. We sway
like lit thuribles.

The clang of vesper bells echoes,
stretches like a shadow on the street,
ricochets off perse clouds.

Do you see the stars?
Swelling and popping
like bloated balloons?

They fall and fizz,
seep through my fingers
onto your bare chest.

BELIEVE IN WHAT IT ISN'T BELIEVE IN WHAT IT ISN'T

house is a carcass & you hid
in its ribs fed on an organ's bruise
i crawl inside myself again this body
occupied by many mouths you said home exists
only in memory— separation of body
from body every night i pray
between home & here
like a parasite you exhaust my entrails
you tear me to pieces will skin forget?

SELF-PORTRAIT WITH FIRE

stars scar-white fall
            like teeth

sky is a sleeping mouth   a bruised neck—
and who wouldn't want to bruise the sky?

      my body is mute:
a mountain, the moon-
         flower blooming in December dark—

but this forest is on fire   swells
my mouth held open for the ashfall

I swallow smoke—

      my body holds a secret

—I am always becoming

THE DARKER HALF OF THE YEAR

After birth, a mother goat eats the placenta to hide
her child from wolves—rebirth through refuge.

Night writes itself around me,
carves my name in clay.

Bloodless womb, altar of hands,
swollen breasts, curdled milk.

To an empty sky I pray,
scrap my skin's blurred sentences—
this unspeakable grammar.

I've never held anything
in my hands long enough to watch it grow.

What I mean is, I hold moth to candle,
let wax & wing dissolve into flame.

What I mean is, in the end we all fall,
ashes to ashes, muscle to dust, or something like it.

THE UNGARDENING

Fields grow numb with winter.
Through pines, the throaty pink
hour of evening staggers,
like a sleepy child heavy on her feet.

Need I remind you?
All that's still once fell.

In the garden, a maple unwrites
scarlet letters to dusk.
Forget-me-nots frost
and fall to the hard ground.
Birds fly in a V to somewhere warmer.

Here's the bedroom: empty chest
of drawers, raw mattress,
flowers wilt on the windowsill.

Like January,
you came and went,
benumbing the earth,
ungardening all I planted.

AUGUST IN GEORGIA IS A PIGEON-PALE FIELD BLOOMING

And here we are,
nestled between two haystacks—
needles with no want for thread.

Each night, another star dies,
the remains settle onto our spines
like dust on an unused porch.

Locusts swarm this time of year,
yet we run wolf-wild through open fields.

If my body were a map, would you pin me to your bedroom wall? Mark red X's where you'd want to explore?
(How about here, and here?)

Stirrupless, the last star slips
from the sky, falls into dirt.
You brush it off, press it into my palm.

This is where the hours hang
heavy with owls. The sky, a bruise, purples.

Still, your body, like the land, goes:

        cornfield, cornfield, cliff—

a farmland forgotten,
feet loam-stained, taprooting.

TONGUE, ENDANGERED

Years ago, our language thawed,
each letter pressed against my chest.

Now, I feel you in exhales—
collage of trees fathered by wind.

The almost-animal in me folds
a memory of our room in half.

I sit in the corner with unswept
sunlight & spiders, hungry

for your voice. I am one word
too many, a bruise factory,

unapologetic for the noun
of my body. My hips,

parenthesis. Not even the maple
can look away. But you,

you are the wonderful one,
smile like a C-section scar,

mouthing the river blue,
never making a noise.

LITANY OF DEPARTURES

        Afterdamp of April, evening thaws.
A hungry mutt
           yowls a bruised gospel,

      its body a dying star—
throat aflame with want.
        Night thickens

      with the reek of things unwanted
by heaven. An owl calls to a hole
          in the sky where the moon once fit.

      Wolves circle this village,
snatch blind children mid-street.
          Lord, make me the hound

      that crawls beneath the porch to rot.
Let me return home, alone,
          unravel each worn ligament

from bone, dissolve
        into this tilted hour.

NOTES

After Meditating in the Forest – The phrase "Frog rattle" is from an untitled fragment by Lorine Niedecker and "wounded doe" is from her poem "Wilderness."

Moksgm'ol - The Spirit Bear, known as *Moksgm'ol* ("White Bear") by local First Nations, is a rare subspecies of black bear born with white fur. Spirit bears inhabit ancient rainforests on the northwest coast of British Columbia.

On Nights When I Am Motherless – "Asking Her Father Where Her Mother Went" by Christina Mun-Lutz inspired this poem.

Phayom – *Phayom* (Thai: พยอม, or *shorea roxburghii*, is an endangered semievergreen tree species native to Cambodia, India, Laos, Malaysia, Myanmar, Thailand, and Vietnam.

Sapria Himalayana – *Sapria Himalayana* is an endangered holoparasitic flowering plant species whose primary host is the woody vine known as tetrastigma. *Sapria Himalayana* is a rare plant that grows in the Eastern Himalayas.

Tsuku Tsuku Boshi – *Meimuna opalifera*, known in Japan as tsuku-tsuku-boshi, is a cicada named for its summer song. These cicadas emerge in July and are no longer seen by about October.

ACKNOWLEDGMENTS

Grateful acknowledgment is made to the following publications, in which some of these poems, sometimes in different forms, first appeared: *Atticus Review*, *Damselfly Press*, *DIAGRAM*, *Dialogist*, *Elke: A Little Journal*, *Glass: A Journal of Poetry*, *Gulf Stream Literary Magazine*, *Hermeneutic Chaos Journal*, *Lullwater Review*, *Milk Journal*, *The Mindful Word*, *Rogue Agent*, *So To Speak*, *Tooth n Nail*, and *Wildness Magazine*.

Thank you to the University of South Florida, the Stadler Center for Poetry, the Bucknell Seminar for Undergraduate Poets, and Eckerd College's Writers in Paradise for providing me with the time, space, and resources to write this chapbook.

I am deeply grateful to Jay Hopler and Christina Mun-Lutz for guiding me toward, through, and with poetry; Ylce Irizarry and Ira Sukrungruang for their instruction in the early drafts of this chapbook; all of my instructors and classmates at USF, especially Amanda Sharon, Erika Goodrich, Gabriella Ramirez, and Courtney Boswell. I'm also grateful and honored to have had the opportunity to attend workshops with the following visiting instructors at USF: Naomi Shihab Nye, Terrance Hayes, Kimberly Johnson, Sandra Beasley, and Maurice Manning.

Thank you to Campbell McGrath and my poetry workshop group at Writers in Paradise for taking me further into the wonderful world of Poetry Land.

To Jonathan Simkins, J'lyn Chapman, Emma Bolden, Robert Eric Shoemaker, Jay Hopler, and Christina Mun-Lutz: thank you for taking the time to read this book and for offering your generous and thoughtful words in the form of blurbs.

I'm forever grateful to the June Poets of 2016: Daniel Barnum, Nora Claire Miller, Nikolina Lazetic, Tanner Pruitt, Caroline Schmidt, Tom Kozlowski, Tobi Kassim, Reilly D. Cox, Helena Chung, Christian Wessels, Abby MacGregor, and our instructors and mentors Katie Hays, Chet'la Sebree, Emily Means, Deirdre O'Connor, Mary Jo Bang, Brian Teare, and Tori Dikeman, our year's honorary Junie. I will always cherish that beautiful and unforgettable summer we all spent together.

I want to express my deepest gratitude to everyone at the Jack Kerouac School of Disembodied Poetics, as well as other friends and instructors at Naropa University, the Summer Writing Program, the Boulder Writers Warehouse, and our Front Range community as a whole. Thank you all for your endless inspiration, guidance, and love.

A special thank you to Chelsea Dingman for encouragement, insight, friendship, and collaboration. You are a poetry guardian angel.

To Joseph Braun, Indigo Deany, and The Lune: Thank you, thank you, thank you for believing in this work and handling it with such gentle, caring hands and hearts. Thank you for offering my words this special space.

I am eternally grateful to my family, especially my parents, for always encouraging me to follow my heart and to be open to all the universe has to offer.

And lastly, thank you to my biggest fan and most fierce supporter, my husband Hector. Gracias por tu música, tus historias, y tu amor.

ABOUT THE AUTHOR

Sarah Alcaide-Escue is a wanderer/wonderer from the swamplands of Central Florida. She earned her MFA in Creative Writing and Poetics from Naropa University and has earned fellowships from the Jack Kerouac School of Disembodied Poetics, the Bucknell Seminar for Undergraduate Poets, & Eckerd College's Writers in Paradise. She's a poetry editor at *The Adirondack Review* and daylights as a copywriter and amateur herbalist.

www.ingramcontent.com/pod-product-compliance
Lightning Source LLC
Chambersburg PA
CBHW071323080526
44587CB00018B/3334